Ten Mistakes of Israel

Sadhu Prasad

Publisher

Fantabulous Publishers India

www.fantabulous.co.in

Edition: 2024

©Copyright: Sadhu Prasad

Ten Mistakes of Israel

Penned by Sadhu Prasad

Published by Fantabulous Publishers India

Introduction

Israel's position in the Middle East has been one of constant challenge and adaptation since its establishment in 1948. From its inception, Israel has been surrounded by adversaries and faced with complex geopolitical realities that have shaped its policies and actions. While Israel has often been praised for its resilience and ingenuity in navigating these challenges, it has also made significant mistakes that have had far-reaching consequences for the region.

In this book, we embark on a journey to examine ten critical mistakes that Israel has made in the realm of geopolitics. These mistakes are not intended to discredit Israel or undermine its achievements but rather to provide a nuanced understanding of the challenges it has faced and the lessons that can be drawn from its experiences.

As we delve into each mistake, we will strive to present a balanced and evidence-based analysis, drawing on historical facts, expert opinions, and firsthand accounts. Our goal is not to assign blame but to foster a deeper understanding of the complexities of geopolitics in the Middle East and to explore how Israel's decisions have influenced regional dynamics.

Through this exploration, we hope to shed light on the opportunities for growth and improvement that lie ahead for Israel and its neighbors. By learning from past mistakes and embracing a spirit of introspection and humility, Israel can better navigate the challenges of the future and contribute to the stability and prosperity of the Middle East.

Join us as we unravel the complexities of Israel's geopolitical landscape and uncover the lessons that can be gleaned from its past missteps. Together, we will embark on a journey of discovery and enlightenment, seeking to chart a course towards a more peaceful and prosperous future for all.

Chapter 1: Ignoring Palestinian Nationalism

From its inception, Israel's relationship with the Palestinian people has been complex and contentious. One critical mistake that Israel made early on was underestimating the strength of Palestinian nationalism and the significance of the Palestinian cause. This miscalculation had far-reaching consequences, contributing to prolonged conflict and hindering efforts for peace in the region.

Birth of Israel

To grasp the gravity of Israel's misstep in underestimating Palestinian nationalism, it's imperative to delve into the historical backdrop against which Israel emerged. The year 1948 marked a pivotal moment in the Middle East, as the United Nations Partition Plan paved the way for the establishment of the state of Israel. While this decision was celebrated by Jewish communities worldwide, it sparked profound turmoil among the Palestinian population.

In the wake of the partition, hundreds of thousands of Palestinians were displaced from their ancestral homes, a cataclysmic event etched into Palestinian collective memory as the Nakba, meaning "catastrophe." The scars of dispossession and displacement inflicted deep wounds within Palestinian society, fostering a profound sense of injustice and resentment that reverberates to this day.

The Nakba was not merely a historical event but a defining moment that shaped Palestinian identity and fueled the emergence of Palestinian nationalism. As Palestinians grappled with the trauma of displacement, a fervent desire for self-determination and reclaiming their homeland took root. The Nakba became a rallying cry for generations of Palestinians, symbolizing their enduring struggle for justice and recognition.

However, Israeli leaders at the time failed to grasp the significance of Palestinian nationalism and the deep-rooted grievances stemming from the Nakba. Instead, they viewed Palestinian resistance through a narrow security lens, perceiving it solely as a threat to the fledgling Jewish state's existence. This fundamental misreading of Palestinian aspirations laid the groundwork for decades of conflict and thwarted peace efforts.

Israel's initial approach to the Palestinian question was marked by a combination of military suppression and attempts to co-opt Palestinian leadership. Rather than acknowledging the legitimacy of Palestinian national aspirations, Israeli authorities sought to undermine Palestinian identity and assert control over the occupied territories. This approach only served to exacerbate tensions and fuel Palestinian resistance against Israeli occupation.

However, Israeli leaders initially failed to recognize the strength and legitimacy of Palestinian nationalism. Instead, they viewed the Palestinian issue primarily through the lens of security, seeing Palestinian resistance as a threat to the existence of the Jewish state. This narrow perspective ignored the underlying grievances of the Palestinian people and failed to address the root causes of the conflict.

As a result, Israel pursued policies that sought to suppress Palestinian nationalism rather than engage with it constructively. This approach only served to deepen Palestinian resentment and fuel resistance against Israeli occupation. The Palestinian Liberation Organization (PLO), founded in 1964, emerged as the primary vehicle for Palestinian national aspirations and resistance against Israeli rule.

The Six-Day War of 1967

The Six-Day War of 1967 stands as a pivotal event in the Israeli-Palestinian conflict, reshaping the geopolitical landscape of the Middle East and exacerbating tensions between Israel and the Palestinian people. Following the war, Israel occupied the West Bank, Gaza Strip, and East Jerusalem, bringing millions of Palestinians under its control. However, rather than recognizing the occupation as a catalyst for Palestinian nationalism, Israeli leaders adopted policies aimed at maintaining control and suppressing dissent, deepening the roots of the conflict.

The occupation of the Palestinian territories presented a profound challenge to the aspirations of the Palestinian people for self-determination and statehood. Millions of Palestinians found themselves living under Israeli military rule, subject to restrictions on their movement, access to resources, and political rights. The occupation fueled resentment and resistance among the Palestinian population, laying the groundwork for the emergence of organized opposition to Israeli rule.

Amidst the occupation, the Palestine Liberation Organization (PLO) emerged as a central force in Palestinian politics, representing the aspirations of the Palestinian people for independence and sovereignty. Led by figures such as Yasser Arafat, the PLO became the vanguard of Palestinian resistance, advocating for the establishment of an independent Palestinian state and the right of return for Palestinian refugees. The PLO's call for armed struggle against Israeli occupation resonated deeply with Palestinians, galvanizing support for their cause both domestically and internationally.

However, Israeli leaders dismissed the PLO as a terrorist organization, refusing to engage in meaningful dialogue or negotiations with its leadership. Instead, Israel pursued a policy of military crackdowns and targeted assassinations against PLO operatives, seeking to quash Palestinian resistance through force. This approach only served to deepen

Palestinian resentment and fuel further acts of violence against Israeli targets.

The refusal to engage with the PLO reflected a broader unwillingness on the part of Israeli leaders to acknowledge the legitimacy of Palestinian national aspirations. Instead of viewing the PLO as a legitimate representative of the Palestinian people, Israeli leaders sought to delegitimize and marginalize the organization, portraying it as a threat to Israel's security and existence.

The dismissal of the PLO as a partner for peace negotiations contributed to a prolonged stalemate in the Israeli-Palestinian conflict, with neither side willing to make concessions or engage in meaningful dialogue. Despite occasional attempts at peace talks, including the Oslo Accords of the 1990s, the fundamental issues underlying the conflict remained unresolved, perpetuating a cycle of violence and mistrust.

The failure to recognize the PLO as a legitimate interlocutor for peace negotiations represented a missed opportunity for Israel to address the root causes of the conflict and seek a just and lasting resolution. By refusing to engage with the PLO, Israeli leaders perpetuated a cycle of violence and instability, deepening the animosity between Israelis and Palestinians and prolonging the suffering of both peoples.

In hindsight, the refusal to engage with the PLO can be seen as a critical mistake on the part of Israeli leaders, one that contributed to the perpetuation of the Israeli-Palestinian conflict. By dismissing the legitimate grievances and aspirations of the Palestinian people, Israel missed an opportunity to pursue a path of reconciliation and peace. Recognizing the importance of dialogue and negotiation with all relevant stakeholders is essential for achieving a just and lasting resolution to the Israeli-Palestinian conflict, one that respects the rights and aspirations of both Israelis and Palestinians.

The Oslo Accords (1990 and 1993)

The Oslo Accords of the 1990s emerged as a beacon of hope in the longstanding Israeli-Palestinian conflict, offering a framework for negotiations between Israel and the Palestine Liberation Organization (PLO) aimed at achieving a peaceful resolution. However, despite initial optimism, the Oslo process faltered, revealing deep-seated obstacles to peace, including Israel's failure to fully acknowledge and address Palestinian national aspirations.

The Oslo Accords, signed in 1993, represented a historic breakthrough in Israeli-Palestinian relations, marking the first time both parties formally recognized each other's existence and agreed to negotiate towards a comprehensive peace agreement. Under the accords, Israel recognized the PLO as the legitimate representative of the Palestinian people, while the PLO renounced terrorism and committed to resolving the conflict through peaceful means.

Despite these promising developments, the Oslo process encountered numerous challenges that ultimately undermined its success. One of the key factors contributing to the failure of Oslo was Israel's reluctance to fully acknowledge and address the core grievances of the Palestinian people, including their aspirations for statehood and self-determination.

While the Oslo Accords established a framework for negotiations, they failed to provide a clear path towards the establishment of an independent Palestinian state. Instead, the accords deferred critical issues, such as the status of Jerusalem, the right of return for Palestinian refugees, and the future of Israeli settlements in the occupied territories, to be addressed in later negotiations.

Israel's failure to fully address Palestinian national aspirations during the Oslo process was compounded by its continued expansion of settlements in the occupied territories. Despite commitments under Oslo to freeze settlement construction, Israel continued to expand its presence in the West Bank and Gaza Strip, further entrenching its control over Palestinian land and resources.

The expansion of Israeli settlements not only violated the spirit of the Oslo Accords but also undermined confidence in the peace process among Palestinians. Settlement expansion was widely viewed as a deliberate attempt by Israel to alter the demographic and geographic realities on the ground, making the prospect of a viable Palestinian state increasingly remote.

Moreover, the expansion of settlements fueled Palestinian perceptions of Israeli intransigence and occupation, reinforcing the belief that Israel was not genuinely committed to ending the occupation and achieving a just and lasting peace. As settlement construction accelerated, so too did Palestinian frustration and disillusionment with the Oslo process, ultimately eroding public support for negotiations with Israel.

The failure of Oslo to deliver on its promise of peace highlighted the need for a more comprehensive and inclusive approach to resolving the Israeli-Palestinian conflict. Rather than deferring critical issues to future negotiations, a successful peace process must address the root causes of the conflict upfront, including Palestinian national aspirations and Israeli settlement expansion.

Moving forward, achieving a just and lasting peace will require genuine commitment from both Israel and the Palestinians to engage in meaningful dialogue and negotiation. This includes recognizing and respecting the legitimate rights and aspirations of both peoples, as well as addressing the underlying grievances that have fueled decades of conflict and suffering.

While the Oslo Accords ultimately fell short of achieving their intended goals, they nevertheless represented an important milestone in the pursuit of peace in the Middle East. By learning from the mistakes of Oslo and adopting a more inclusive and proactive approach to peacemaking, Israel and the Palestinians can still chart a path towards a future of peace, security, and mutual coexistence.

Peace negotiations: A Fact-Based Analysis

Peace negotiations between Israelis and Palestinians have been a recurring theme in the turbulent history of the Middle East. Over the decades, various attempts have been made to broker a lasting peace agreement, yet the conflict persists, marked by cycles of violence and stalled negotiations. In this analysis, we delve into the intricacies of peace negotiations between Israelis and Palestinians, examining the historical context, key agreements, and the challenges that have hindered progress towards a comprehensive resolution.

Historical Context:

The Israeli-Palestinian conflict traces its roots back to the late 19th and early 20th centuries, with the emergence of competing national movements among Jews and Arabs in the land then known as Palestine. The establishment of the state of Israel in 1948, following the Arab-Israeli War, led to the displacement of hundreds of thousands of Palestinians, igniting a conflict that has persisted for generations.

Since then, numerous attempts have been made to resolve the conflict through diplomacy and negotiation. Key milestones include the Camp David Accords of 1978, which led to a peace treaty between Israel and Egypt, and the Oslo Accords of the 1990s, which laid the groundwork for Israeli-Palestinian peace negotiations.

Peace Agreements:

The Oslo Accords, signed in 1993, represented a historic breakthrough in Israeli-Palestinian relations. Under the accords, Israel recognized the Palestine Liberation Organization (PLO) as the legitimate representative of the Palestinian people, while the PLO recognized Israel's right to exist and renounced terrorism. The accords also established a framework for negotiations aimed at achieving a two-state solution, with the creation of a Palestinian interim self-government authority in the West Bank and Gaza Strip.

Despite the initial optimism surrounding the Oslo Accords, the peace process faltered in the years that followed. Issues such as the status of Jerusalem, the right of return for Palestinian refugees, and the future of Israeli settlements in the occupied territories proved to be insurmountable obstacles to reaching a comprehensive peace agreement.

Subsequent peace negotiations, including the Camp David Summit of 2000 and the Annapolis Conference of 2007, also failed to yield lasting results. The inability of both sides to reach consensus on key issues, coupled with escalating violence and continued settlement expansion, further undermined prospects for peace.

Challenges and Obstacles:

The Israeli-Palestinian conflict is characterized by deep-seated distrust and animosity between the two sides, rooted in decades of violence, occupation, and competing national narratives. The failure to address core grievances, such as Palestinian statehood and Israeli security concerns, has hindered progress towards a resolution.

One of the central challenges to peace negotiations is the issue of Israeli settlements in the occupied territories. Israel's continued expansion of settlements in the West Bank and East Jerusalem has been a major point of contention, undermining Palestinian trust in the peace process and exacerbating tensions on the ground.

Another obstacle to peace is the lack of unity among Palestinian factions. The division between the Palestinian Authority, which governs the West Bank, and Hamas, which controls the Gaza Strip, has further complicated efforts to negotiate a comprehensive peace agreement. The inability of Palestinians to present a unified front has weakened their bargaining position and limited their ability to negotiate effectively with Israel.

Conclusion:

Despite decades of peace negotiations, the Israeli-Palestinian conflict remains unresolved, with no clear path forward towards a comprehensive peace agreement. The challenges are numerous and complex, ranging from territorial disputes and security concerns to deep-seated distrust and competing national narratives.

Moving forward, achieving a lasting peace will require bold leadership, genuine commitment to dialogue and negotiation, and a willingness to confront the difficult issues that have long divided Israelis and Palestinians. Only through sincere and sustained efforts can the two sides hope to bridge their differences and forge a future of peace, security, and prosperity for all.

Take home Message:

Analyzing Israel's mistake of ignoring Palestinian nationalism offers important insights into the challenges of peacemaking in the Middle East. By recognizing the legitimate aspirations of the Palestinian people and engaging in genuine dialogue and negotiation, Israel can begin to address the root causes of the conflict and move towards a future of peace and reconciliation. Ignoring Palestinian nationalism only perpetuates the cycle of violence and instability, underscoring the importance of a more inclusive and empathetic approach to conflict resolution.

Chapter 2: Settlement Expansion

Israel's policy of settlement expansion in the occupied territories stands as one of the most contentious and enduring issues in the Israeli-Palestinian conflict. Since the Six-Day War in 1967, Israel has pursued a strategy of building and expanding settlements in the West Bank, East Jerusalem, and the Gaza Strip, territories captured during the conflict. This policy has been a major obstacle to peace negotiations, inflaming tensions with the Palestinians and drawing international condemnation. In this chapter, we delve into the history, impact, and implications of Israel's settlement expansion on the prospects for peace in the region.

Historical Context

The roots of Israel's settlement enterprise can be traced back to the immediate aftermath of the Six-Day War. Following Israel's victory in the war, it gained control over the West Bank, East Jerusalem, and the Gaza Strip, territories that are home to a significant Palestinian population. In the years that followed, Israel began establishing settlements in these areas, citing security concerns and biblical and historical ties to the land.

The first Israeli settlement in the West Bank, Kfar Etzion, was established in September 1967, just months after the end of the war. Over the years, the number of settlements grew steadily, with successive Israeli governments providing financial incentives and subsidies to encourage Jewish Israelis to move to the occupied territories.

Impact on Peace Negotiations

Israel's policy of settlement expansion has had profound implications for the prospects of achieving a negotiated settlement to the Israeli-Palestinian conflict. One of the key obstacles to peace negotiations has been the expansion of settlements into territory that Palestinians claim as part of their future state. As settlements have expanded, they have fragmented Palestinian territory, making the establishment of a contiguous and viable Palestinian state increasingly difficult.

The establishment and expansion of settlements have also led to the displacement of Palestinians from their homes and land, exacerbating tensions and fueling resentment among the Palestinian population. In many cases, Palestinian communities have been forcibly evicted to make way for new settlement construction, leading to accusations of human rights abuses and violations of international law.

Moreover, settlements have been a major source of friction and violence between Israelis and Palestinians. The presence of Israeli settlers in the occupied territories has led to clashes with Palestinian residents, as well as attacks on Palestinian property and agricultural land. These incidents have further eroded trust between the two sides and undermined efforts to build confidence and goodwill.

International Condemnation:

Israel's policy of settlement expansion has drawn widespread condemnation from the international community, which views the settlements as illegal under international law. The Fourth Geneva Convention, which governs the treatment of civilians in times of war, prohibits the transfer of civilian populations into occupied territory, a provision that has been interpreted as prohibiting Israel's settlement activities.

Numerous United Nations Security Council resolutions have condemned Israel's settlement expansion, including Resolution 2334, adopted in December 2016, which declared that Israeli settlements in the occupied territories have no legal validity and constitute a flagrant violation of international law. The international community has called on Israel to halt all settlement construction and dismantle existing settlements as a precondition for peace negotiations.

Despite international condemnation, Israel has continued to expand its settlements in the occupied territories, defying calls for a halt to construction. Israeli leaders argue that settlements are necessary for Israel's security and that Jews have a historical and biblical right to live in the land of Israel. They also point to the Oslo Accords, which they argue did not explicitly prohibit settlement construction.

However, critics argue that Israel's settlement policy undermines the prospects for a two-state solution to the Israeli-Palestinian conflict. The expansion of settlements makes it increasingly difficult to establish a contiguous and viable Palestinian state, as well as undermines the territorial integrity of any future Palestinian state. Moreover, settlements contribute to the entrenchment of the occupation and perpetuate the cycle of violence and conflict between Israelis and Palestinians.

Conclusion

Israel's policy of settlement expansion in the occupied territories has been a major obstacle to peace negotiations, inflaming tensions with the Palestinians and drawing international condemnation. The expansion of settlements undermines the prospects for achieving a negotiated settlement to the Israeli-Palestinian conflict, as well as exacerbates the suffering of the Palestinian people. Moving forward, resolving the issue of settlements will be essential for building trust and creating the conditions necessary for a just and lasting peace in the region.

Chapter 3: Lack of Strategic Vision in Lebanon

Israel's involvement in Lebanon, particularly its ill-fated invasion in 1982, stands as a pivotal moment in the history of the Israeli-Palestinian conflict and the broader geopolitics of the Middle East. This chapter delves into the historical context, motivations, consequences, and the lack of strategic vision that characterized Israel's intervention in Lebanon, shedding light on the complexities and ramifications of this military entanglement.

Historical Context

The roots of Israel's involvement in Lebanon can be traced back to the late 1960s and early 1970s, when Palestinian militant groups, such as the Palestine Liberation Organization (PLO), established bases in southern Lebanon from which to launch attacks against Israel. These attacks, which targeted Israeli civilians and military personnel, posed a significant security threat to Israel and contributed to growing tensions along the Israeli-Lebanese border.

In response to the Palestinian presence in Lebanon, Israel conducted a series of military incursions and operations aimed at dismantling PLO infrastructure and preventing cross-border attacks. These operations, which included airstrikes, artillery barrages, and commando raids, resulted in significant casualties on both sides and fueled animosity between Israel and Lebanon.

Motivations for the Invasion

Israel's decision to invade Lebanon in 1982 was driven by a combination of strategic, political, and security considerations. One of the primary motivations behind the invasion was to remove the threat posed by the PLO and its militant allies, who had established a de facto state-within-a-state in southern Lebanon and continued to launch attacks against Israel.

In addition to addressing the security threat posed by the PLO, Israeli leaders also sought to weaken and undermine the influence of the Syrian regime, which had long supported and sheltered Palestinian militants in Lebanon. By intervening in Lebanon, Israel hoped to assert its dominance in the region and send a message to its adversaries that it would not tolerate threats to its security.

Furthermore, the invasion of Lebanon was driven by domestic political considerations, including the desire to bolster the popularity of then-Israeli Prime Minister Menachem Begin and his right-wing Likud party. Begin portrayed the invasion as a preemptive strike against terrorism and framed it as a necessary step to ensure the security and survival of the Israeli state.

Consequences of the Invasion:

The Israeli invasion of Lebanon in 1982 had far-reaching and profound consequences for both Israel and Lebanon, as well as the wider Middle East region. The invasion, which was initially intended to be a limited military operation, quickly escalated into a full-scale war that lasted for months and resulted in tens of thousands of casualties.

One of the most tragic outcomes of the invasion was the massacre of Palestinian refugees in the Sabra and Shatila refugee camps in Beirut. Following the assassination of Lebanese President-elect Bashir Gemayel, Israeli-allied Lebanese Christian militias entered the camps and carried out a brutal campaign of violence and killings, resulting in the deaths of an estimated 800 to 3,500 civilians.

The massacre at Sabra and Shatila drew international condemnation and led to widespread outrage both within Israel and around the world. Many Israelis were shocked and dismayed by the actions of their government and military, leading to protests and calls for accountability. The massacre also tarnished Israel's reputation on the international stage and raised questions about the morality and legality of its actions in Lebanon.

Furthermore, the invasion failed to achieve its stated objectives of removing the PLO from Lebanon and establishing a stable security buffer along Israel's northern border. While the PLO was eventually forced to evacuate

Beirut and relocate to Tunisia, it continued to operate in other parts of Lebanon and remained a potent force in the region.

Moreover, the invasion deepened sectarian divisions within Lebanon and contributed to the outbreak of a brutal and protracted civil war that lasted for more than a decade. The war, which pitted various Lebanese factions against each other and drew in regional powers such as Syria and Iran, resulted in widespread destruction, displacement, and loss of life.

Lack of Strategic Vision

One of the critical mistakes of Israel's intervention in Lebanon was the lack of a clear strategic vision and exit strategy. While the invasion succeeded in weakening the PLO and temporarily bolstering Israel's security, it ultimately led to a prolonged and costly military entanglement that strained Israel's resources and undermined its international standing.

Israeli leaders failed to anticipate the complexities and challenges of occupying and administering southern Lebanon, which was home to a diverse array of ethnic and religious communities. The lack of a coherent plan for post-invasion governance and reconstruction allowed sectarian tensions to escalate and created fertile ground for the rise of militant groups such as Hezbollah, which emerged as a powerful adversary to Israel in the years that followed.

Furthermore, the invasion exacerbated tensions with Israel's Arab neighbors and strained its relationships with key allies, such as the United States. The disproportionate use of force and civilian casualties during the invasion sparked outrage and condemnation from the international community, undermining Israel's credibility as a responsible actor on the world stage.

Conclusion

Israel's invasion of Lebanon in 1982 was a watershed moment in the history of the Israeli-Palestinian conflict and the broader geopolitics of the Middle East. Driven by a combination of strategic, political, and security considerations, the invasion had far-reaching and profound consequences for both Israel and Lebanon, as well as the wider region.

The lack of a clear strategic vision and exit strategy was a critical mistake that ultimately undermined the success of Israel's intervention in Lebanon. While the invasion succeeded in weakening the PLO and temporarily bolstering Israel's security, it ultimately led to a prolonged and costly military entanglement that strained Israel's resources, undermined its international standing, and deepened divisions within Lebanon.

Moving forward, it is essential for policymakers to learn from the mistakes of the past and adopt a more cautious and pragmatic approach to managing conflicts in the region. A clear strategic vision, informed by a comprehensive understanding of the complexities and challenges on the ground, is essential for achieving long-term stability and security in the Middle East. Only through dialogue, negotiation, and compromise can the cycle of violence and conflict be broken, paving the way for a future of peace and prosperity for all.

Chapter 4: Failure to Achieve Lasting Peace with Egypt

Israel's peace treaty with Egypt in 1979 marked a historic milestone in the turbulent history of the Middle East. However, despite this significant achievement, the failure to address the underlying issues of the Israeli-Palestinian conflict has prevented the Israeli-Egyptian peace treaty from leading to a broader regional peace. In this chapter, we explore the complexities, challenges, and opportunities in Israeli-Egyptian peace, focusing on the need to address the Israeli-Palestinian conflict for lasting regional stability.

Historical Context:

The peace treaty between Israel and Egypt, known as the Camp David Accords, was signed in September 1978, following months of negotiations brokered by the United States. The treaty, which was mediated by then-US President Jimmy Carter, represented the first-ever peace agreement between Israel and an Arab state, ending decades of hostility and conflict between the two sides.

Under the terms of the treaty, Israel agreed to withdraw its military forces from the Sinai Peninsula, which it had occupied since the Six-Day War in 1967, in exchange for full diplomatic recognition and normalized relations with Egypt. The treaty also established a framework for resolving other outstanding issues between the two countries, including the demarcation of their shared border and the normalization of economic and cultural ties.

Challenges in Implementing Peace:

While the Israeli-Egyptian peace treaty was a significant breakthrough, its implementation faced numerous challenges and obstacles. One of the primary challenges was the need to overcome decades of mutual hostility and suspicion between Israel and Egypt, which had fought four major wars since the founding of the Israeli state in 1948.

The normalization of relations between Israel and Egypt was met with resistance from within both countries, particularly from hardline factions opposed to reconciliation with the enemy. In Israel, right-wing political parties and settler groups opposed the withdrawal from Sinai, viewing it as a betrayal of Jewish sovereignty over the biblical land of Israel. In Egypt, nationalist and Islamist groups accused President Anwar Sadat of capitulating to Israeli demands and abandoning the Palestinian cause.

Another challenge was the need to address the economic and security concerns of both parties in the aftermath of the peace treaty. The withdrawal of Israeli forces from Sinai created a security vacuum in the region, leading to concerns about the potential for terrorist attacks and cross-border infiltrations. To address these concerns, Israel and Egypt negotiated security arrangements, including the deployment of international peacekeeping forces and the demilitarization of certain areas along the border.

Opportunities for Regional Peace:

Despite the challenges and obstacles, the Israeli-Egyptian peace treaty created opportunities for broader regional cooperation and reconciliation. The normalization of relations between Israel and Egypt paved the way for increased economic and cultural exchanges, as well as cooperation in areas such as tourism, trade, and technology.

The peace treaty also served as a model for future peace efforts in the region, demonstrating that Arab-Israeli conflict could be resolved through negotiation and diplomacy rather than military force. Inspired by the success of the Camp David Accords, other Arab states, such as Jordan and the United Arab Emirates, later followed suit and signed peace treaties with Israel, furthering the cause of regional stability and cooperation.

However, the failure to address the underlying issues of the Israeli-Palestinian conflict has prevented the Israeli-Egyptian peace treaty from fulfilling its potential as a catalyst for broader regional peace. While Israel and Egypt have enjoyed relatively stable and peaceful relations since signing the treaty, the unresolved Palestinian question continues to cast a shadow over the region, fueling tensions and preventing true reconciliation between Israelis and Arabs.

Importance of Addressing the Israeli-Palestinian Conflict:

The Israeli-Palestinian conflict lies at the heart of the broader Arab-Israeli conflict and represents one of the most significant barriers to achieving lasting peace and stability in the Middle East. The failure to resolve the conflict has led to decades of violence, suffering, and instability, impacting the lives of millions of Israelis and Palestinians alike.

The ongoing occupation of Palestinian territories, the expansion of Israeli settlements, and the lack of progress towards a negotiated settlement have all contributed to the perpetuation of the conflict. The absence of a viable Palestinian state alongside Israel undermines the prospects for regional peace and security, fueling resentment and radicalization among Palestinians and other Arab populations.

Addressing the Israeli-Palestinian conflict is essential for unlocking the full potential of Israeli-Egyptian peace and achieving broader regional stability. A comprehensive and just resolution to the conflict, based on the principles of international law and UN resolutions, is necessary to address the legitimate aspirations and grievances of both Israelis and Palestinians and pave the way for a future of peace, security, and prosperity for all.

Conclusion:

While Israel's peace treaty with Egypt in 1979 was a significant achievement, its failure to address the underlying issues of the Israeli-Palestinian conflict has prevented it from leading to a broader regional peace. The normalization of relations between Israel and Egypt created opportunities for cooperation and reconciliation, but the unresolved Palestinian question continues to cast a shadow over the region, fueling tensions and preventing true reconciliation between Israelis and Arabs.

Moving forward, addressing the Israeli-Palestinian conflict must be a top priority for regional peace efforts. A comprehensive and just resolution to the conflict, based on the principles of international law and UN resolutions, is necessary to unlock the full potential of Israeli-Egyptian peace and achieve lasting stability and security in the Middle East. Only through genuine dialogue, negotiation, and compromise can the cycle of violence and conflict be broken, paving the way for a future of peace and prosperity for all.

Chapter 5: Mishandling the Gaza Strip

Israel's approach to the Gaza Strip has been a subject of intense scrutiny and debate, both within Israel and internationally. This chapter delves into the historical context, motivations, consequences, and challenges of Israel's policies towards the Gaza Strip, including its blockade and military incursions. It examines how these policies have impacted the population of Gaza, exacerbated tensions, and hindered efforts to achieve lasting peace in the region.

Historical Context:

The Gaza Strip, a narrow coastal enclave located on the eastern coast of the Mediterranean Sea, has been a focal point of the Israeli-Palestinian conflict for decades. Following the 1948 Arab-Israeli War, Gaza came under Egyptian control until the Six-Day War in 1967, when Israel occupied the territory along with the West Bank, East Jerusalem, and the Golan Heights.

Since then, Gaza has remained under Israeli military occupation, with Israel controlling its borders, airspace, and territorial waters. In 2005, Israel unilaterally withdrew its military forces and dismantled its settlements in Gaza, a move that was hailed as a step towards peace. However, Israel maintained control over Gaza's borders, restricting the movement of goods and people in and out of the territory.

In 2007, the situation in Gaza took a dramatic turn when the militant group Hamas seized control of the territory in a violent coup, ousting the rival Fatah faction, which controlled the Palestinian Authority. Since then, Gaza has been governed by Hamas, which Israel, the United States, and the European Union consider a terrorist organization.

Israel's Approach to Gaza:

Israel's approach to Gaza has been characterized by a combination of military force, economic blockade, and diplomatic isolation. In response to rocket attacks launched from Gaza by Hamas and other militant groups, Israel has conducted numerous military operations and airstrikes targeting militants and infrastructure in the territory.

In addition to military action, Israel has imposed a blockade on Gaza, restricting the flow of goods and humanitarian aid into the territory. The blockade, which has been in place since 2007, has had a devastating impact on Gaza's economy and infrastructure, leading to widespread poverty, unemployment, and shortages of essential goods such as food, medicine, and electricity.

Israel defends its blockade of Gaza as a necessary security measure aimed at preventing Hamas from acquiring weapons and materials that could be used to attack Israel. Israeli officials argue that the blockade is not aimed at punishing the civilian population of Gaza but rather at weakening Hamas and preventing it from launching attacks against Israel.

However, critics argue that Israel's blockade of Gaza constitutes collective punishment and violates international law. The United Nations and human rights organizations have condemned the blockade as a form of collective punishment, which is prohibited under international humanitarian law. They argue that the blockade has caused immense suffering and hardship for the civilian population of Gaza, who are already living under difficult conditions due to the ongoing conflict and Israeli occupation.

Consequences of Israel's Policies:

Israel's policies towards Gaza have had far-reaching and profound consequences for the population of the territory, as well as for regional stability and security. The blockade has led to a humanitarian crisis in Gaza, with widespread poverty, unemployment, and food insecurity. According to the United Nations, more than half of Gaza's population lives below the poverty line, and unemployment rates are among the highest in the world.

Moreover, the blockade has severely restricted access to essential services such as healthcare, education, and clean water, exacerbating the suffering of the civilian population. Hospitals in Gaza are chronically understaffed and under-resourced, and medical supplies are in short supply, leading to preventable deaths and suffering among the sick and injured.

The blockade has also hindered reconstruction efforts in Gaza, following years of conflict and destruction. Israel's military operations and airstrikes have caused widespread damage to Gaza's infrastructure, including homes, schools, hospitals, and water and sanitation facilities. However, the blockade has prevented the importation of construction materials and other essential goods needed for rebuilding, leaving much of Gaza in ruins.

Furthermore, Israel's military incursions into Gaza have resulted in civilian casualties and widespread destruction, further fueling resentment and hostility towards Israel. The use of disproportionate force and the targeting of civilian infrastructure have been condemned by the international community as violations of international law and humanitarian principles.

Challenges and Opportunities for Peace:

Israel's policies towards Gaza have exacerbated tensions and hindered efforts to achieve lasting peace in the region. The blockade has deepened the sense of despair and hopelessness among the population of Gaza, fueling radicalization and extremism. The ongoing cycle of violence and conflict between Israel and Gaza has further entrenched divisions and hindered efforts to build trust and confidence between the two sides.

However, despite the challenges, there are also opportunities for peace and reconciliation. The recent ceasefire agreements between Israel and Hamas, brokered by Egypt and other mediators, have provided temporary relief from the violence and offered a glimmer of hope for a more lasting peace. These agreements have included provisions for easing restrictions on the movement of goods and people in and out of Gaza, as well as for rebuilding Gaza's infrastructure and economy.

Moving forward, achieving lasting peace in Gaza will require a comprehensive and inclusive approach that addresses the underlying grievances of the population, including the lifting of the blockade, the reconstruction of Gaza's infrastructure, and the promotion of economic development and job creation. It will also require renewed efforts to revive the peace process and address the broader Israeli-Palestinian conflict, including the establishment of a viable Palestinian state alongside Israel.

Conclusion:

Israel's approach to Gaza, including its blockade and military incursions, has failed to address the underlying grievances of the population and has only served to exacerbate tensions. The blockade has led to a humanitarian crisis in Gaza, with widespread poverty, unemployment, and food insecurity. The ongoing cycle of violence and conflict between Israel and

Gaza has further entrenched divisions and hindered efforts to achieve lasting peace in the region.

Moving forward, achieving peace in Gaza will require a comprehensive and inclusive approach that addresses the legitimate concerns and aspirations of both Israelis and Palestinians. This includes lifting the blockade, easing restrictions on the movement of goods and people, and promoting economic development and job creation in Gaza. It also requires renewed efforts to revive the peace process and address the broader Israeli-Palestinian conflict, paving the way for a future of peace, security, and prosperity for all.

Chapter 6: Alienating Potential Allies

Israel's diplomatic relations have been a critical aspect of its foreign policy strategy since its establishment in 1948. However, its approach to diplomacy has faced scrutiny and criticism, both domestically and internationally. This chapter delves into the historical context, motivations, consequences, and challenges of Israel's diplomatic approach, examining how it has alienated potential allies in the region and around the world and hindered efforts to garner international support for its policies.

Historical Context:

Israel's diplomatic challenges stem from its unique position in the Middle East as a Jewish-majority state in a predominantly Arab and Muslim region. Since its inception, Israel has faced hostility and rejection from many of its Arab neighbors, who have refused to recognize its legitimacy and have sought to undermine its existence through military, political, and diplomatic means.

In response to these challenges, Israel has pursued a range of diplomatic strategies aimed at securing its position in the region and gaining international recognition and support. These strategies have included forging alliances with non-Arab states, such as the United States and European countries, as well as engaging in peace negotiations with its Arab neighbors, such as Egypt and Jordan.

However, Israel's diplomatic efforts have often been hampered by its perceived heavy-handed approach to diplomacy, which has alienated potential allies and fueled resentment and opposition to its policies.

Motivations and Consequences:

Israel's approach to diplomacy has been shaped by a range of factors, including security concerns, historical grievances, and ideological considerations. Israeli leaders have often adopted a confrontational and assertive stance in their dealings with other states, viewing diplomacy through the lens of national security and survival.

One of the key motivations behind Israel's diplomatic approach has been the need to counter perceived threats to its security and existence. Israel has faced numerous security challenges since its establishment, including wars, terrorist attacks, and threats of annihilation from hostile neighbors. In response, Israeli leaders have prioritized security concerns in their diplomatic engagements, often adopting a zero-sum mentality that prioritizes Israel's interests above all else.

However, this approach has often alienated potential allies and partners in the region and around the world. Israel's uncompromising stance on issues such as the Israeli-

Palestinian conflict, settlements, and human rights has led to tensions and disagreements with key allies, including the United States and European countries, as well as with Arab and Muslim states.

Moreover, Israel's policies towards the Palestinians, including its occupation of the West Bank and blockade of Gaza, have drawn widespread condemnation from the international community, undermining its credibility and legitimacy on the world stage. The United Nations, human rights organizations, and many foreign governments have criticized Israel's actions as violations of international law and humanitarian principles, further isolating Israel diplomatically and eroding its support among the international community.

Challenges and Opportunities:

Israel's diplomatic challenges are multifaceted and complex, reflecting the deep-seated divisions and conflicts in the Middle East. However, they also present opportunities for reflection, reevaluation, and renewal in Israel's approach to diplomacy.

One of the key challenges facing Israel is the need to rebuild trust and confidence with its neighbors and potential allies in the region. This will require a willingness to engage in meaningful dialogue and negotiation, as well as a willingness to make concessions and compromises in pursuit of peace and stability.

Another challenge is the need to address the root causes of the Israeli-Palestinian conflict and work towards a comprehensive and just resolution. This will require Israel to demonstrate a commitment to ending the occupation, halting settlement expansion, and respecting the rights and dignity of the Palestinian people. By addressing the grievances of the Palestinians and working towards a two-state solution, Israel can help alleviate regional tensions and build bridges with its neighbors.

Furthermore, Israel must work to repair its relations with key allies and partners in the international community, including the United States and European countries. This will require a more nuanced and balanced approach to diplomacy, one that takes into account the concerns and interests of other states and seeks to build consensus and cooperation on shared challenges and opportunities.

Conclusion:

Israel's approach to diplomacy has faced numerous challenges and obstacles, both domestically and internationally. Its sometimes heavy-handed approach has alienated potential allies in the region and around the world, making it more difficult to garner international support for its policies.

Moving forward, Israel must adopt a more nuanced and balanced approach to diplomacy, one that prioritizes dialogue, negotiation, and cooperation over confrontation and conflict.

By addressing the root causes of the Israeli-Palestinian conflict, rebuilding trust and confidence with its neighbors, and repairing its relations with key allies, Israel can help create the conditions for lasting peace and stability in the Middle East.

Chapter 7: Overreliance on Military Solutions

Israel's strategic posture has frequently leaned heavily on military solutions to address complex political challenges, a tendency that has perpetuated a cycle of violence and instability in the region. This chapter explores the historical context, motivations, consequences, and ramifications of Israel's reliance on military strategies, providing an analytical discussion on the implications of this approach.

Historical Context:

Since its establishment in 1948, Israel has faced a multitude of security threats, both internal and external. The constant threat of conflict with neighboring Arab states, as well as the challenge of Palestinian resistance, has shaped Israel's security doctrine and influenced its approach to addressing political challenges.

Israel's military capabilities, honed through decades of conflict and warfare, have played a central role in shaping its national security strategy. The Israel Defense Forces (IDF), one of the most technologically advanced and well-equipped militaries in the world, has been tasked with defending the country's borders, deterring potential adversaries, and responding to security threats.

Motivations and Consequences:

Israel's reliance on military solutions to address political challenges can be attributed to a range of factors, including security concerns, historical grievances, and strategic imperatives. Israeli leaders have often viewed military force as a necessary and effective means of safeguarding the country's security and preserving its territorial integrity.

One of the key motivations behind Israel's military-centric approach is the perceived existential threat posed by its adversaries, particularly hostile Arab states and militant groups such as Hezbollah and Hamas. Israeli leaders have sought to deter aggression and prevent attacks through a combination of military deterrence, preemptive strikes, and targeted assassinations.

However, this reliance on military force has had profound consequences for Israel and the wider region. The use of military solutions to address political challenges has often exacerbated tensions, fueled radicalization, and perpetuated a cycle of violence that has hindered efforts to achieve lasting peace and stability.

Moreover, Israel's military operations, particularly in the occupied territories, have resulted in civilian casualties, widespread destruction, and human rights abuses. The use of disproportionate force, collective punishment, and the targeting of civilian infrastructure have drawn condemnation from the international community and undermined Israel's moral and legal standing.

Challenges and Opportunities:

Israel's overreliance on military solutions poses significant challenges for its security and stability, as well as for regional peace and security. The militarization of Israeli society, fueled by decades of conflict and insecurity, has led to a culture of violence and aggression that perpetuates the cycle of conflict and undermines efforts to achieve a political resolution to the Israeli-Palestinian conflict.

One of the key challenges facing Israel is the need to shift away from a purely military-centric approach to addressing political challenges and towards a more holistic and nuanced strategy that incorporates diplomacy, dialogue, and conflict resolution. This will require a willingness to engage with adversaries and explore diplomatic solutions to long-standing conflicts, as well as a commitment to respecting international law and human rights principles.

Furthermore, Israel must address the root causes of the Israeli-Palestinian conflict, including the occupation of Palestinian territories, the expansion of settlements, and the lack of political rights and self-determination for Palestinians. By addressing these grievances and working towards a just and lasting resolution to the conflict, Israel can help alleviate tensions and create the conditions for peace and stability in the region.

Conclusion:

Israel's overreliance on military solutions to address political challenges has perpetuated a cycle of violence and instability in the region. While security concerns are legitimate and real, the militarization of Israeli society and the continued use of force to address political challenges have undermined efforts to achieve lasting peace and security.

Moving forward, Israel must adopt a more balanced and nuanced approach to addressing political challenges, one that incorporates diplomacy, dialogue, and conflict resolution alongside military force. By addressing the root causes of conflict and working towards a just and lasting resolution to the Israeli-Palestinian conflict, Israel can help create the conditions for peace and stability in the region.

Chapter 8: Failure to Address Socioeconomic Disparities

Israel's failure to effectively address socioeconomic disparities within its own society has emerged as a significant challenge, impacting both domestic stability and its ability to project stability externally. This chapter examines the historical context, root causes, consequences, and potential solutions to the socioeconomic disparities in Israel, providing an analytical discussion on the implications of this failure.

Historical Context:

Since its establishment in 1948, Israel has made significant strides in economic development and prosperity, transforming itself from a predominantly agrarian society into a modern, industrialized nation. However, despite its economic success, Israel continues to grapple with persistent socioeconomic disparities that have widened in recent years.

The roots of these disparities can be traced back to various factors, including historical inequalities, geopolitical challenges, demographic changes, and government policies. The influx of Jewish immigrants from diverse cultural and socioeconomic backgrounds, coupled with the influx of Palestinian refugees and the ongoing conflict with the Arab states, has created complex social and economic dynamics within Israeli society.

Moreover, Israel's security concerns and defense expenditures have placed a significant strain on its economy, diverting resources away from social welfare programs and exacerbating socioeconomic inequalities. The rapid growth of high-tech industries and the globalization of the economy have also contributed to widening income disparities and disparities in access to education, healthcare, and housing.

Root Causes and Consequences:

The failure to adequately address socioeconomic disparities in Israel can be attributed to a range of structural, institutional, and policy-related factors. These include inadequate investment in education, healthcare, and social welfare programs, as well as discriminatory practices and policies that have marginalized certain segments of the population, including Arab Israelis, ultra-Orthodox Jews, and other minority groups.

The consequences of these disparities are far-reaching and profound, impacting various aspects of Israeli society, including social cohesion, political stability, and economic growth. Socioeconomic inequalities have fueled resentment, alienation, and frustration among marginalized communities, leading to social unrest, protests, and even violence in some cases.

Moreover, socioeconomic disparities have weakened Israel's ability to project stability externally, undermining its credibility and legitimacy on the world stage. The perception of Israel as a prosperous and egalitarian society has been tarnished by reports of poverty, inequality, and social injustice, leading to criticism and condemnation from the international community.

Challenges and Opportunities:

Addressing socioeconomic disparities in Israel is a complex and multifaceted challenge that requires a comprehensive and coordinated approach. One of the key challenges is overcoming entrenched social, cultural, and political barriers that have perpetuated inequalities and discrimination. This will require a commitment to promoting social justice, equality, and inclusion, as well as investment in education, healthcare, and social welfare programs.

Furthermore, Israel must address the root causes of socioeconomic disparities, including discriminatory practices and policies that have marginalized certain segments of the population. This will require political will, leadership, and vision to enact meaningful reforms and address the structural and institutional barriers that perpetuate inequalities.

Moreover, Israel must harness the talents and potential of all its citizens, regardless of their background or socioeconomic status. This will require investment in education, skills training, and economic development programs that empower individuals and communities to participate fully in the economic and social life of the country.

Conclusion:

Israel's failure to adequately address socioeconomic disparities within its own society has emerged as a significant challenge, impacting both domestic stability and its ability to project stability externally. Addressing these disparities requires a comprehensive and coordinated approach that addresses the root causes of inequality, promotes social justice and inclusion, and invests in education, healthcare, and social welfare programs.

Moving forward, Israel must prioritize efforts to reduce socioeconomic disparities, promote social cohesion and inclusion, and empower marginalized communities to participate fully in the economic and social life of the country. By addressing these challenges, Israel can strengthen its domestic stability, enhance its credibility and legitimacy on the world stage, and contribute to a more prosperous and equitable future for all its citizens.

Chapter 9: Neglecting Soft Power

Israel's approach to soft power, or the ability to shape perceptions and win hearts and minds through cultural, diplomatic, and humanitarian means, has been a subject of critique and analysis. This chapter delves into the historical context, motivations, consequences, and opportunities of Israel's neglect of soft power, providing an analytical discussion on the implications of this oversight.

Historical Context:

Since its inception in 1948, Israel has grappled with the complexities of its image and reputation on the international stage. Positioned in a volatile region amidst ongoing conflict, Israel has often relied on military strength and strategic alliances to secure its interests and protect its security.

However, the importance of soft power in shaping global perceptions and fostering international support has become increasingly apparent in the modern era of diplomacy and information warfare. Soft power encompasses cultural influence, diplomatic engagement, and humanitarian efforts, all of which play a crucial role in shaping public opinion and winning over allies and supporters.

Motivations and Consequences

Israel's neglect of soft power can be attributed to various factors, including a focus on security concerns, a reliance on military solutions, and a lack of strategic vision in shaping its international image. Israeli leaders have often prioritized hard power over soft power, viewing military strength and strategic alliances as the primary means of ensuring Israel's security and survival.

However, this approach has had unintended consequences, undermining Israel's credibility and legitimacy on the world stage. The perception of Israel as a militarized and aggressive state has fueled criticism and condemnation from the international community, eroding support for Israel and strengthening the position of its adversaries.

Moreover, Israel's neglect of soft power has allowed its adversaries, particularly Palestinian groups and other Arab states, to gain the upper hand in the battle for public opinion. By leveraging cultural, diplomatic, and humanitarian initiatives, Israel's adversaries have been able to shape global perceptions and garner sympathy and support for their cause.

Challenges and Opportunities

Addressing Israel's neglect of soft power presents a range of challenges and opportunities. One of the key challenges is overcoming entrenched attitudes and perceptions that have shaped Israel's approach to diplomacy and public relations. This will require a shift in mindset and strategy, one that recognizes the importance of soft power in shaping global perceptions and fostering international support.

Moreover, Israel must invest in cultural, diplomatic, and humanitarian initiatives that promote its values, achievements, and contributions to the world. By showcasing its vibrant culture, technological innovation, and commitment to democracy and human rights, Israel can enhance its soft power and win over hearts and minds around the world.

Furthermore, Israel must engage with diverse audiences and stakeholders, including civil society organizations, international institutions, and the media, to effectively communicate its message and counteract negative narratives. By engaging in dialogue, building relationships, and promoting mutual understanding, Israel can strengthen its soft power and build alliances based on shared values and interests.

Conclusion

Israel's neglect of soft power has undermined its credibility and legitimacy on the world stage, allowing adversaries to gain the upper hand in the battle for public opinion. Addressing this oversight requires a shift in mindset and strategy, one that recognizes the importance of soft power in shaping global perceptions and fostering international support.

Moving forward, Israel must invest in cultural, diplomatic, and humanitarian initiatives that promote its values, achievements, and contributions to the world. By engaging with diverse audiences and stakeholders, Israel can effectively communicate its message and build alliances based on shared values and interests. By harnessing the power of soft power, Israel can strengthen its position on the world stage and secure its interests in an increasingly interconnected and complex global landscape.

Chapter 10: Lack of Long-Term Strategic Planning

Israel's geopolitical decisions have been shaped by a multitude of factors, ranging from security concerns to regional dynamics. However, a critical aspect that has often been overlooked is the lack of long-term strategic planning. This chapter delves into the historical context, motivations, consequences, and potential solutions regarding Israel's deficiency in long-term strategic planning, providing an analytical discussion on the implications of this oversight.

Historical Context:

Since its establishment in 1948, Israel has navigated a complex and volatile geopolitical landscape, characterized by conflicts, alliances, and shifting power dynamics. The country's strategic imperatives have been shaped by its unique geopolitical position in the Middle East, surrounded by hostile neighbors and facing persistent security threats.

Despite these challenges, Israel has often responded to immediate threats and crises with short-term, tactical measures, rather than adopting a long-term, strategic approach to addressing its security and diplomatic challenges. This lack of long-term planning has left Israel vulnerable to unforeseen developments and has hindered its ability to effectively advance its interests on the regional and global stage.

Motivations and Consequences

The lack of long-term strategic planning in Israeli geopolitics can be attributed to various factors, including the country's focus on immediate security concerns, domestic political dynamics, and a tendency towards risk aversion. Israeli leaders have often prioritized short-term gains over long-term strategic objectives, opting for tactical responses to crises rather than developing comprehensive, forward-looking strategies.

However, this approach has had significant consequences for Israel's security, stability, and international standing. By failing to anticipate and prepare for future challenges, Israel has found itself ill-equipped to navigate shifting geopolitical dynamics and emerging threats. This has resulted in missed opportunities, strategic setbacks, and a lack of coherence in Israel's foreign policy approach.

Moreover, the lack of long-term strategic planning has undermined Israel's credibility and legitimacy on the world stage, as the country's actions have been perceived as reactive and ad-hoc, rather than strategic and visionary. This has eroded trust and confidence in Israel's ability to effectively manage regional conflicts and contribute to regional stability.

Challenges and Opportunities

Addressing Israel's lack of long-term strategic planning presents a range of challenges and opportunities. One of the key challenges is overcoming the short-term mindset that has dominated Israeli politics and decision-making processes. This will require a shift in mindset and culture, one that values strategic foresight, planning, and preparedness over short-term expediency.

Moreover, Israel must develop a comprehensive, forward-looking strategy that anticipates future challenges and identifies opportunities for advancing its interests on the regional and global stage. This will require input from a wide range of stakeholders, including policymakers, military experts, intelligence analysts, and civil society organizations.

Furthermore, Israel must invest in the development of strategic thinking and planning capabilities within its government institutions, military, and academic institutions. By building a cadre of strategic planners and analysts, Israel can better anticipate and respond to emerging threats and opportunities, and develop proactive strategies to advance its long-term interests.

Conclusion:

Israel's lack of long-term strategic planning in geopolitics has hindered its ability to effectively navigate the complex and volatile regional landscape. Addressing this deficiency requires a shift in mindset, culture, and capabilities, towards a more strategic, forward-looking approach to decision-making and policy formulation.

Moving forward, Israel must invest in the development of strategic thinking and planning capabilities within its government institutions, military, and academic institutions. By fostering a culture of strategic foresight, planning, and preparedness, Israel can better anticipate and respond to emerging threats and opportunities, and develop proactive strategies to advance its long-term interests on the regional and global stage.

Conclusion

Conclusion: Learning from Israel's Geopolitical Mistakes Israel's journey through the intricate geopolitics of the Middle East has been marked by a series of challenges, successes, and, importantly, mistakes. Acknowledging and learning from these mistakes is imperative for the nation to chart a more secure and prosperous future, not only for itself but also for the entire region. This conclusion reflects on the significant lessons gleaned from Israel's geopolitical missteps and emphasizes the importance of implementing sound policies to achieve its objectives while fostering peace and stability in the Middle East.

Reflection on Past Mistakes:

Throughout its history, Israel has encountered various obstacles in its pursuit of security, stability, and recognition in the region. From its failure to adequately address Palestinian nationalism to its reliance on military solutions and neglect of soft power, Israel's geopolitical landscape has been fraught with challenges that have shaped its trajectory and influenced its standing on the global stage.

The tendency to prioritize short-term gains over long-term strategic planning has often left Israel vulnerable to unforeseen developments and hindered its ability to effectively address complex political challenges. This lack of foresight has not only undermined Israel's credibility and legitimacy but also perpetuated a cycle of conflict and instability in the region.

Furthermore, Israel's approach to diplomacy and public relations has sometimes alienated potential allies and fueled resentment and opposition to its policies. The failure to effectively engage with diverse audiences and stakeholders has weakened Israel's position on the world stage and hindered its ability to garner international support for its objectives.

The Way Forward:

Moving forward, Israel must heed the lessons learned from its geopolitical mistakes and adopt a more nuanced and strategic approach to navigating the complexities of the Middle East. This entails recognizing the importance of addressing underlying grievances, promoting dialogue and reconciliation, and investing in diplomatic, cultural, and humanitarian initiatives to foster trust and cooperation.

Furthermore, Israel must prioritize long-term strategic planning and foresight in its decision-making processes, taking into account the broader implications of its actions and policies. By adopting a more proactive and forward-looking approach, Israel can better anticipate and respond to emerging threats and opportunities, and develop comprehensive strategies to advance its interests on the regional and global stage.

Moreover, Israel must invest in building bridges with its neighbors and fostering regional cooperation and integration. By engaging in dialogue and cooperation with Arab states, Israel can help build a more stable and prosperous Middle East, where peace and prosperity are achievable for all.

Final note:

In conclusion, Israel's geopolitical journey has been fraught with challenges and mistakes, but it is through recognizing and learning from these mistakes that the nation can chart a more secure and prosperous future. By adopting a more nuanced and strategic approach to geopolitics, prioritizing long-term planning and foresight, and investing in dialogue and cooperation, Israel can better position itself to achieve its objectives while promoting peace and stability in the Middle East. As the nation moves forward, it is essential to remain vigilant, adaptable, and committed to building a brighter future for generations to come.

Ten Mistakes of Israel

Sadhu Prasad

Publisher

Fantabulous Publishers India

www.fantabulous.co.in

Edition: 2024

©Copyright: Sadhu Prasad

Ten Mistakes of Israel

Penned by Sadhu Prasad

Published by Fantabulous Publishers India

Popular Story and Activity Books for Children

Fanta-Award Recipients

(All Books available on Amazon-Worldwide and in Google as eBook)…